CINCINNATI
BENGALS

by Marty Gitlin

Published by ABDO Publishing Company, 8000 West 78th Street, Edina, Minnesota 55439. Copyright © 2011 by Abdo Consulting Group, Inc. International copyrights reserved in all countries. No part of this book may be reproduced in any form without written permission from the publisher. SportsZone™ is a trademark and logo of ABDO Publishing Company.

Printed in the United States of America,
North Mankato, Minnesota
062010
092010

THIS BOOK CONTAINS AT LEAST 10% RECYCLED MATERIALS.

Editor: Matt Tustison
Copy Editor: Nicholas Cafarelli
Interior Design and Production: Marie Tupy
Cover Design: Marie Tupy

Photo Credits: Thomas Witte/AP Images, cover; NFL Photos/AP Images, title page, 27; AP Images, 4, 7, 8, 12, 15, 16, 19, 42 (top), 42 (middle), 42 (bottom); Paul Spinelli/AP Images, 11; Kathy Willens/AP Images, 20; Al Behrman/AP Images, 23, 33, 35, 36, 38, 41, 43 (top), 43 (middle), 43 (bottom), 47; Maribeth Joeright/AP Images, 24; David Stluka/AP Images, 28, 31; Rusty Kennedy/AP Images, 44

Library of Congress Cataloging-in-Publication Data
Gitlin, Marty.
  Cincinnati Bengals / Marty Gitlin.
    p. cm.—(Inside the NFL)
  Includes index.
  ISBN 978-1-61714-007-5
  1. Cincinnati Bengals (Football team)—History—Juvenile literature. I. Title.
  GV956.C6G57 2011
  796.332'640977178—dc22
                              2010013678

TABLE OF CONTENTS

CHAPTER 1

ARCTIC BLAST

I t was not just cold in Cincinnati that day in 1982. It was the coldest January 10 in the city's history. The thermometer told the story: nine degrees below zero. Freezing winds howled through Riverfront Stadium. The wind chill dipped to a numbing minus 59 degrees. And many of the Bengals played in short-sleeve shirts.

It was the 1981 American Football Conference (AFC) Championship Game. The freezing visitors from sunny and warm California were the San Diego Chargers. The Bengals had never won a playoff game until a 28–21 victory over the

FIRST, ONLY CATCH

Bengals receiver Don Bass sure picked a good time to grab his first catch of the 1981 season. His 3-yard snag of a pass from quarterback Ken Anderson was the touchdown that clinched the AFC championship against San Diego. Bass never caught another pass in the NFL.

CINCINNATI QUARTERBACK KEN ANDERSON CALLS A PLAY IN THE AFC TITLE GAME IN JANUARY 1982. THE WIND CHILL REACHED MINUS 59 DEGREES.

DÉJÀ VU FOR FORREST GREGG

As the Bengals prepared for the AFC title game, coach Forrest Gregg shared with them some words of wisdom. He told them that playing in the bitter cold was like going to the dentist. "You know it's going to hurt, but you got to go anyway," he said.

Gregg knew all about dealing with the cold. He spent his playing career as an offensive lineman with the Green Bay Packers, who often played in freezing conditions.

He had played in weather just as fierce during the 1967 NFL Championship Game. It was 13 below zero at Lambeau Field when his Packers defeated the Dallas Cowboys 21–17 in the "Ice Bowl."

Through 2009, the Ice Bowl remained the coldest game in NFL history in terms of air temperature. The wind chill of minus 48 degrees, however, was not as low as the minus 59 degrees reached in the 1981 AFC Championship Game.

Buffalo Bills the week before. A win on this icy, blustery afternoon would send them to their first Super Bowl.

It was no contest. The Bengals took a 17–0 lead in the first half. They allowed just one touchdown to the Chargers. San Diego had been averaging 29.9 points per game. That was the most in the National Football League (NFL). Cincinnati's defense intercepted two passes and forced two fumbles.

Bengals battering-ram running back Pete Johnson—all 250 pounds of him—rushed for 80 yards and a touchdown. Quarterback Ken Anderson threw for two more touchdowns.

The Bengals returned to the locker room with a 27–7

COACH FORREST GREGG IS CARRIED OFF THE FIELD AFTER THE BENGALS ADVANCED TO THE SUPER BOWL IN JANUARY 1982.

ter," offered *Sports Illustrated* writer Ron Fimrite. "Cincinnati's defense frustrated the Chargers every bit as often as the wind and the chill."

There would be no chill to overcome two weeks later at the Bengals' next game. They played the rugged San Francisco 49ers indoors in Super Bowl XVI in Pontiac, Michigan.

But there would be a stingy 49ers defense to overcome—and the Bengals could not do it. Trailing 20–7 late in the third quarter, they drove all the way to San Francisco's 1-yard line. But with the goal line very close, they were stopped on four straight plays.

The Bengals never truly recovered. Anderson threw a touchdown pass to tight end

win. They could finally warm up while they celebrated an AFC title. Defensive end Eddie Edwards had a frostbitten left ear.

Meanwhile, the media began typing up glowing reports. They wrote about how the Bengals dominated the Chargers in what later became known as the Freezer Bowl.

"The fact is the Bengals were just tougher, smarter and bet-

THE 49ERS STOP THE BENGALS' PETE JOHNSON (46) AT THE GOAL LINE IN THE THIRD QUARTER OF SUPER BOWL XVI. SAN FRANCISCO WON 26–21.

was held to 36 yards on 14 carries by the 49ers.

Still, the 26–21 defeat failed to diminish the team's accomplishment. Cincinnati had never even won a playoff game heading into the season.

That is not to say that the Bengals took a lot of time to become competitive after playing their first season in 1968. They got good in a hurry.

Dan Ross to cut the deficit to 20–14. But two 49ers field goals put the game out of reach. Ross made another touchdown catch with 16 seconds left in the game. By that time, though, the Bengals were doomed.

They had ridden the back of the powerful Johnson all year. But not on this Super Bowl Sunday. Johnson had rushed for 1,077 yards during the regular season. On this day, however, he

FORMER CINCINNATI TACKLE ANTHONY MUNOZ, SHOWN IN 1984, IS CONSIDERED ONE OF THE GREATEST OFFENSIVE LINEMEN IN NFL HISTORY.

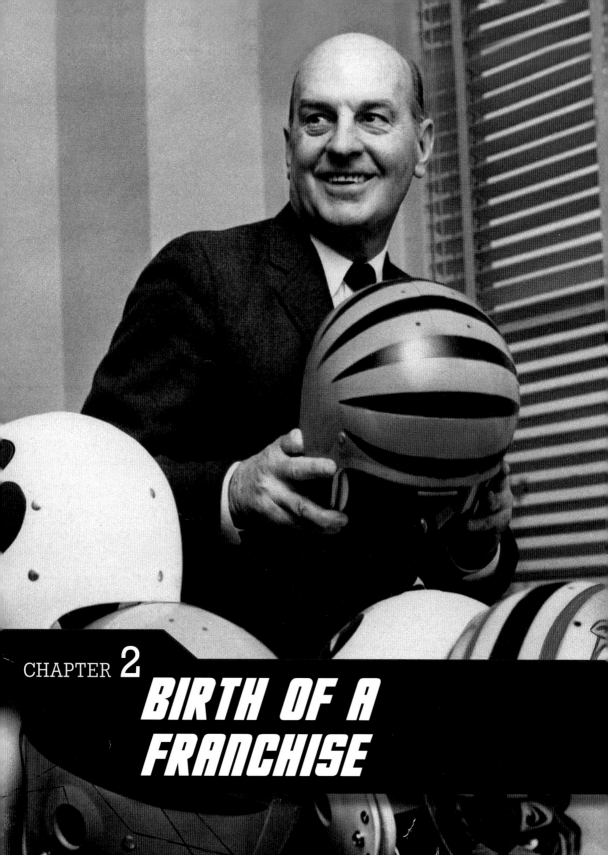

CHAPTER 2

BIRTH OF A FRANCHISE

Paul Brown was getting antsy by the mid-1960s. The former standout coach of the Cleveland Browns had been fired by that team after the 1962 season. He wanted to get back into football.

Brown's son, Mike, studied possible pro football expansion cities and recommended Cincinnati. Paul met with Ohio Governor James Rhodes. The governor agreed that the state could make room for two teams. Soon the American Football League (AFL) awarded a franchise to Cincinnati. A merger with the NFL had already been planned and took place in 1970.

The new team decided to adopt the nickname of a Cincinnati team that had played in the 1930s—the Bengals. Paul Brown

THEY ONLY LIKED HOME COOKING

One reason the Bengals struggled during their first two-and-a-half years is that they could not win on the road. From their inception in 1968 to the middle of the 1970 season, their record away from Cincinnati was 1–16–1.

PAUL BROWN, WHO HAD COACHED THE CLEVELAND BROWNS, WAS THE OWNER AND COACH OF THE NEW CINCINNATI BENGALS FRANCHISE IN 1968.

was not only the new team's coach, but also its owner.

Expansion teams generally need several years to become respectable. It appeared the Bengals were following the typical path. They won two of their first three games in their first season in 1968. Then they lost 10 of their final 11. They won their first three games in 1969, but just one more during the rest of the season. So when they dropped six of their first seven in 1970, it seemed as if the team was still not ready to be a contender. Then a strange thing happened. The Bengals started to win. The offense began to pay frequent visits to the end zone. The defense, which had been trampled all season, was stopping foes dead in their tracks. The Bengals won their last seven games, outscoring their opponents by an average of 30–11.

The last victory was a 45–7 rout of the Boston Patriots. That sent the Bengals into the playoffs. But perhaps nearly as satisfying to Paul Brown was a 14–10 win over the Browns, the team that bore his name. Brown had been angered by his firing in 1962, so the win over Cleveland provided some revenge.

THE BENGALS' PAUL ROBINSON (18) SCORES THE GO-AHEAD TOUCHDOWN IN CINCINNATI'S 14–10 WIN OVER CLEVELAND ON NOVEMBER 15, 1970.

"For us, that was a very keen rivalry," said Mike Brown, who later took over for his father as team owner. "Nobody said anything, but everybody understood that (Cleveland) game was a little bit like the Army-Navy (a college football rivalry). That's the one that mattered; the others were important, but this one was more important.

". . . Throughout my father's time here, especially when he was coach here . . . games [against Cleveland] were meaningful, special games. And we took them very seriously."

They took the playoff game very seriously as well. However, the young Bengals lost to the rugged Baltimore Colts 17–0. Despite that defeat, it had become obvious that Brown had

VERY SPECIAL TEAMS

The first of the Bengals' seven straight victories to end the 1970 regular season featured a strange twist. The defense and special teams scored 37 points in the 43–14 win over the Buffalo Bills. The hero was Lemar Parrish, who scored on a 95-yard kickoff return and an 83-yard return of a blocked field goal. Defensive end Royce Berry scored on an 8-yard fumble return. Place-kicker Horst Muhlmann added 19 points on five field goals and four extra points.

turned the team around. The Bengals had only one more losing season through 1977 and qualified for the playoffs again in 1973 and 1975.

Brown guided the team to a sparkling 11–3 record in 1975. Still, that season ended with a 31–28 playoff loss at Oakland. The Bengals rallied to score two touchdowns in the fourth quarter. But they fell short of victory.

CINCINNATI'S ISAAC CURTIS BEATS OAKLAND'S NEAL COLZIE TO GATHER IN A TOUCHDOWN PASS IN THE BENGALS' 31–28 PLAYOFF LOSS IN 1975.

FROM BUCKEYES TO BENGALS

Sometimes a player's talent does not translate from college football into the NFL. Such was the case with running back Archie Griffin.

Griffin had performed brilliantly with the Ohio State Buckeyes. In fact, he remains the only athlete ever to twice win the Heisman Trophy, the award presented to the top college football player every year.

The Bengals picked Griffin late in the first round of the 1976 NFL Draft. He had been passed over by many scouts who believed he boasted neither the speed nor the size to thrive as a professional. And they were right. Though he performed well at times, Griffin never rushed for more than 700 yards in a season before retiring in 1982.

In 2010, son Adam, a running back/defensive back, signed to follow in his father's footsteps at Ohio State. Archie is still tied to Ohio State as alumni association president.

"I was proud of my team," Brown said after the game. "They never quit."

Instead, Brown quit. He retired in 1975, never to return to the sideline. However, he remained the team's owner. By that time, the Bengals had reached the playoffs three times but had lost each time in the first round. The 1981 Super Bowl year would break that string. After that, the Bengals began a period in which they played well at times and poorly at others.

STEELERS LINEBACKERS JACK LAMBERT (58) AND JACK HAM BRING DOWN BENGALS RUNNING BACK ARCHIE GRIFFIN IN 1977.

CHAPTER 3

AN INCONSISTENT DECADE

Bengals fans hoped the Super Bowl berth after the 1981 season would lead to a Super Bowl win right around the corner.

Those hopes were quickly dashed. The Bengals qualified again for the playoffs in a 1982 season that featured a long players' strike. Then they settled into mediocrity.

Coach Forrest Gregg left after leading the team to a 7–9 record in 1983. He was replaced by Sam Wyche. The Bengals did only slightly better the next

SPEAKING HIGHLY OF RILEY

The Bengals have boasted a number of talented defensive backs over the years, including six-time Pro Bowl cornerback Lemar Parrish. But when it came to intercepting the football, the most successful was Ken Riley. Riley, who played with the team from 1969 to 1983, still holds a number of team interception records. He intercepted 65 passes during his career, nearly twice as many as any other Bengals player. He also holds the team mark with five interceptions returned for touchdowns.

BOOMER ESIASON LED THE BENGALS TO THE SUPER BOWL IN JANUARY 1989. HE MIGHT BE THE GREATEST QUARTERBACK IN TEAM HISTORY.

QB TO COACH

Most NFL fans remember Sam Wyche as the Bengals' coach from 1984 to 1991. Few recall that he also served as one of the team's quarterbacks from 1968 to 1970.

Wyche had far more success as a coach than as a player. He lost nearly every game he played as a quarterback with the Bengals.

With Wyche as coach, Cincinnati went 10–6, 4–11, 12–4, 8–8, 9–7, and 3–13 from 1986 to 1991.

He was not afraid to speak his mind. Wyche angered Cleveland Browns fans in 1990 when he grabbed the public address microphone during a Bengals game in Cincinnati. He screamed at fans who were throwing snowballs onto the field because they were angry at the officials. "You don't live in Cleveland," Wyche yelled at the fans. "You live in Cincinnati!"

Wyche lost his job with the Bengals after the 1991 season before hooking up with Tampa Bay as coach.

three years before falling to 4–11 in 1987.

There seemed little reason to hope. But just as they did in 1981 after a poor performance in 1980, the Bengals responded in 1988. They won their first six games and easily made the playoffs. After a 21–13 victory over the Seattle Seahawks, they hosted the Buffalo Bills with a Super Bowl berth on the line.

The unlikely hero that season was a running back named Ickey Woods. He captured the imagination of football fans throughout America with the "Ickey Shuffle," a two-step dance he performed after scoring touchdowns.

FORMER BENGALS QUARTERBACK SAM WYCHE COACHED CINCINNATI TO THE SUPER BOWL AFTER THE 1988 SEASON. HE WAS KNOWN FOR BEING OUTSPOKEN.

Woods danced a lot in 1988. He scored 15 touchdowns that season and rushed for 1,066 yards. Woods scored two more touchdowns to help the Bengals defeat the Bills 21–10. He received plenty of help from the defense, which held Buffalo to 45 rushing yards.

The win set up another showdown against San Francisco in the Super Bowl.

Among the Bengals who had participated in the first Super Bowl against the 49ers was wide receiver Cris Collinsworth. And he made it clear that he wanted a different result this time.

"I've got one of those tiny AFC championship rings," Collinsworth said, "and nobody comes to golf tournaments to peek at those little things. They

BRILLIANT BOOMER

The best quarterback in Bengals history? Many would argue that it is Ken Anderson. But it could very well be Boomer Esiason. Esiason played for the Bengals from 1984 to 1992, then again briefly in 1997. He threw for 27,149 yards and 187 touchdowns in that time. He still owns the team record with 23 300-yard games.

want to see that big Super Bowl ring, and I want one."

Collinsworth never would get that Super Bowl ring. The Bengals led 13–6 going into the fourth quarter. However, the 49ers scored two touchdowns to beat Cincinnati again. This time the score was 20–16.

The game-winner was a pass from Joe Montana to John Taylor with just 34 seconds remaining. Montana, who many believe is the greatest quarterback in NFL history, drove his team 92 yards.

CINCINNATI RUNNING BACK ICKEY WOODS DOES THE "ICKEY SHUFFLE" AFTER SCORING A TOUCHDOWN. WOODS BECAME KNOWN FOR THE DANCE.

Rather than lament the defeat, Collinsworth praised Montana.

"We had them on the 8 [-yard line] with three minutes to go," he said, "and somebody came up to me and said, 'We got 'em now.' I said, 'Have you taken a look at who's quarterbacking the San Francisco 49ers?' That's what it comes down to. Joe Montana is not human. I don't want to call him a god, but he's definitely somewhere in between."

Through the 2009 season, the Bengals had not yet returned to the Super Bowl. And in the 1990s, they had the worst overall record in the NFL.

> "... Somebody came up to me and said, 'We got 'em now.' I said, 'Have you taken a look at who's quarterbacking the San Francisco 49ers?' That's what it comes down to. Joe Montana is not human. I don't want to call him a god, but he's definitely somewhere in between."
>
> —Former Bengals wide receiver Cris Collinsworth, on Super Bowl XXIII

THE BENGALS' LEWIS BILLUPS WALKS AWAY AS THE 49ERS CELEBRATE A LATE GO-AHEAD TOUCHDOWN IN THEIR 20–16 SUPER BOWL WIN ON JANUARY 22, 1989.

CHAPTER 4

THE LEAN YEARS

T he 1990s started out just fine for the Bengals. They won enough games in 1990 to qualify for the playoffs. They even defeated the Houston Oilers 41–14 to reach the second round.

And though they were eliminated the next week in a 20–10 loss to the Los Angeles Raiders, there was reason for optimism. After all, they might have won had All-Pro tackle Anthony Munoz not been sidelined with a shoulder injury.

The good feelings went away in a hurry. And they stayed gone

NOT OK AT QB

The quarterback position is probably the most important on any NFL team. One major reason the Bengals struggled in the 1990s was that they could not find a suitable quarterback after Boomer Esiason was traded to the New York Jets in 1993. One quarterback who did enjoy some success during that time was Jeff Blake. Blake started from 1994 to 1997 and again in 1999. His finest seasons were in 1995 and 1996, when he completed 57 percent of his passes and threw for 52 touchdowns.

DAVID KLINGLER THROWS A PASS IN 1993. THE BENGALS HAD THE NFL'S WORST RECORD IN THE 1990s. THEY WENT 52–108.

OFFENSIVE OFFENSE

The 1993 Bengals, who finished with a record of 3–13, had one of the weakest offenses in the history of the NFL. The Bengals featured no running back or wide receiver who gained more than 654 yards. It is no wonder that they scored 187 points all season, an average of 11.7 per game. They did not score more than 21 points in any game that year.

for about 13 years. Owner Paul Brown died just four weeks before the start of the 1991 season. His son Mike took over. The Bengals then began one of the longest strings of disappointments in the history of the NFL.

Sam Wyche was gone as coach after 1991. The team had a 3–13 record that season, the worst in team history. He was replaced by David Shula, son of legendary Baltimore Colts and Miami Dolphins coach Don Shula.

The Bengals' performance under the younger Shula was terrible. They lost 37 of their first 48 games under him and were bad on offense and defense.

The Bengals then showed flashes of respectability. Shula guided the team to a 7–9 record in 1995. After a poor start in 1996, he was replaced by Bruce Coslet. Coslet won seven of his first nine games that year and six of his last eight in 1997. Talented young players such as running back Corey Dillon and wide receiver Carl Pickens brought hope to Cincinnati's suffering fans.

That hope did not last long. Coslet managed just a 7–28 record after 1997 before quitting early in the 2000 season.

BENGALS QUARTERBACKS GENERALLY DID NOT FARE WELL IN THE 1990s. JEFF BLAKE WAS AN EXCEPTION. HE HAD STRONG SEASONS IN 1995 AND 1996.

MASTER OF "D"

Dick LeBeau may have failed to turn the Bengals around when he coached the team from 2000 to 2002. Even so, he has made his mark as a Hall of Fame player and one of the most respected assistant coaches in the NFL.

LeBeau was a standout cornerback for the Detroit Lions in the 1960s and early 1970s. He set an NFL record by playing in 171 straight games at that position. He ranked eighth in league history, through the 2009 season, with 61 interceptions.

He was voted into the Pro Football Hall of Fame in 2010.

LeBeau established himself as arguably the finest defensive coordinator in the NFL with the Pittsburgh Steelers in 1995 and 1996 before returning to that team in 2004. He is known for an aggressive, attacking style. Under him, the Steelers have consistently ranked near the top of the league in quarterback sacks and fewest points allowed.

No NFL team suffered through a worse decade in the 1990s than the Bengals. Their record in those 10 years of 52–108 was the worst in the NFL. The only other NFL team that won fewer than 60 games during that time was the Arizona Cardinals.

After Coslet's departure, defensive lineman John Copeland said that the players should only blame their failures on the men they saw in the mirror.

"There have to be changes," he said. "Each and every player has to change what they are doing. It starts with the players. If we don't do it, it can't be done by anybody else."

COREY DILLON PLAYED FOR SEVERAL LOSING BENGALS TEAMS. HE STILL RUSHED FOR 1,000 YARDS IN EACH OF HIS FIRST SIX NFL SEASONS.

GREATNESS IN THE MIDST OF MISERY

One of the best players ever to perform on a terrible team was Bengals running back Corey Dillon. Dillon wasted no time achieving stardom, rushing for 1,129 yards as a rookie in 1997. He exceeded 1,000 rushing yards in each of the next five seasons despite the fact his team compiled a record of 19–61 during that stretch. He earned a spot on the AFC Pro Bowl team for three years in a row beginning in 1999.

It could not be done by Dick LeBeau, who followed Coslet as coach. The Bengals simply continued to lose, hitting rock bottom with a team-worst 2–14 record in 2002. Mike Brown then hired a promising young coach named Marvin Lewis to take over.

"LeBeau . . . had been no worse than Bruce Coslet before him, who had been no worse than Dave Shula before him," wrote Lonnie Wheeler in a book about the Bengals titled *The Road Back.*

"It's hard to say when the Bengals actually secured their status as the lowliest professional franchise in American sport. The steady plummet had begun in 1991, coincidentally or not the year that Paul Brown passed on. It continued, unabated, and perhaps even deepening, until Mike Brown hired Marvin Lewis in January, 2003."

Fortunes were about to improve dramatically for the Bengals.

QUARTERBACK JON KITNA DOES NOT LIKE A CALL DURING A GAME IN 2002. CINCINNATI FINISHED 2–14 THAT SEASON.

CHAPTER 5

SEEDS OF SUCCESS

The Bengals did so poorly in 2002 that even playing average football seemed like an unrealistic goal as they prepared for the 2003 season.

But they achieved mediocrity that season—and it was a welcome accomplishment. The Bengals lost their first three games under new coach Marvin Lewis before winning eight of their next 11 to finish 8–8. They even made a run at a playoff spot before losing their final two games.

ONE-TWO PUNCH

In 2007, a Bengals receiver tied for the NFL lead in catches with 112. One might assume it was Chad Johnson, but it was T. J. Houshmandzadeh. Johnson did break the team record with 1,440 receiving yards that season. Both earned spots on the AFC Pro Bowl squad. It is no wonder with two such receivers that quarterback Carson Palmer broke personal records with 373 completions and 4,131 passing yards in 2007.

THE BENGALS IMPROVED GREATLY UNDER MARVIN LEWIS, WHO TOOK OVER AS COACH IN 2003. IN 2005, HE LED THEM TO A PLAYOFF BERTH.

CHAD JOHNSON, WHO LATER CHANGED HIS NAME TO CHAD OCHOCINCO, WAS ONE OF CINCINNATI'S YOUNG OFFENSIVE STARS IN THE 2000s.

NEAR MISSES

The Bengals might have made the play-offs four times from 2003 to 2009 if not for two late-season collapses. The Bengals were 8–6 in 2003—Marvin Lewis's first year as coach—but lost their final two games to fall out of contention. They were 8–5 in 2006 but dropped their last three games to miss out on the playoffs.

According to Lonnie Wheeler, who authored a book about the Bengals' return to playing well, Lewis was greatly responsible for the improvement.

"Lewis had to construct a whole new culture in Cincinnati,

where losing had become . . . seemingly inevitable," he wrote. ". . . Whatever was changeable, he changed, whether it was players or practice schedules or dinner menus. He was everywhere, talking to everybody, doing everything. . . . In some cities, 8–8 would be an eminently forgettable season. In Cincinnati, it was practically a miracle."

The Bengals continued to improve. This was mostly due to an explosive offense led by young quarterback Carson Palmer, wide receivers Chad Johnson and T. J. Houshmandzadeh, and running back Rudi Johnson. They repeated the 8–8 finish in 2004, and then improved to 11–5 in 2005. It was their first winning record and playoff berth since 1990.

FROM JOHNSON TO OCHOCINCO

Many things have been said and written about Bengals wide receiver Chad Johnson. But he has never been called boring.

In August 2008, Johnson officially changed his last name to Ochocinco, which means 8–5 in Spanish. He chose the name because he wears No. 85 on his uniform.

He had already earned a reputation for being one of a kind. One time, he sent each Cleveland Browns defensive back a bottle of Pepto Bismol, a medicine used for upset stomachs. That was his way of warning them that he was going to make them sick trying to cover him.

Ochocinco, however, is best known for his touchdown celebrations. Perhaps his most famous was his "marriage proposal." After scoring a touchdown against Indianapolis in 2005, he kneeled down and pretended to be proposing marriage to a Bengals cheerleader.

Luck, however, was not on their side in the first round of the playoffs against the archrival Pittsburgh Steelers. Palmer injured his knee on his first pass when he was hit by the Steelers' Kimo Von Oelhoffen.

"I knew right away that it was bad," Palmer said. "I felt my whole knee pop. . . . It was just a sickening feeling because I knew . . . my season was over."

The Bengals' season was over as well. They showed enough courage to overcome Palmer's injury and take a 17–7 lead, but they could not keep the momentum and lost 31–17.

Lewis understood at that point that his main task was to construct a strong defense, which had been lacking since the late 1980s. The Bengals took a step back the next three years. They dropped to 4–11–1 in 2008 due greatly to an injury that knocked Palmer out for the season. But the defense, led by talented linebackers Dhani Jones, Keith Rivers, and Rashad Jeanty, blossomed in 2009. The result was a 10–6 record and the second playoff berth in five years.

There was no longer any doubt that the Bengals were back as a championship contender. The misery of the 1990s was becoming a distant memory.

QUARTERBACK CARSON PALMER REACTS AFTER HE SUFFERED A KNEE INJURY IN CINCINNATI'S 31–17 PLAYOFF LOSS TO PITTSBURGH ON JANUARY 8, 2006.

TIMELINE

1966	Paul Brown and Ohio Governor James Rhodes make a presentation to bring an AFL franchise to Cincinnati.
1967	Cincinnati is awarded an AFL franchise. The team is named the Bengals.
1970	The Bengals defeat the Boston Patriots 45–7 to earn their first playoff berth in franchise history.
1971	The Bengals select quarterback Ken Anderson in the third round of the NFL Draft.
1973	After a 10–4 season gets them a playoff berth, the Bengals lose a first-round game to Miami, 34–16.
1975	The Bengals compile a franchise-best 11–3 record but fall to Oakland 31–28 in the first round of the playoffs.
1976	Paul Brown retires as coach but remains the owner of the Bengals.
1981	The Bengals win 12 regular-season games to qualify for the playoffs.
1982	After a first-round victory over Buffalo, the Bengals beat San Diego 27–7 in a minus-59 degree wind chill on January 10 to reach their first Super Bowl. They lose 26–21 to San Francisco in the Super Bowl on January 24.

1985	Boomer Esiason is named the starting quarterback. The Bengals score a team-record 441 points during the season.
1988	The Bengals again win 12 games to qualify for the playoffs.
1989	A 21–10 victory over Buffalo on January 8 sends the Bengals into another Super Bowl showdown against San Francisco. On January 22, they are again defeated by the 49ers, 20–16.
1991	Owner Paul Brown dies on August 5, just four weeks before the regular season. He is replaced by son Mike Brown.
2000	The Bengals begin play at the newly constructed Paul Brown Stadium.
2003	New coach Marvin Lewis is hired and begins turning the Bengals around by guiding them to an 8–8 record.
2006	An injury to starting quarterback Carson Palmer plays a big role in a 31–17 first-round playoff loss to Pittsburgh on January 8.
2010	After going 10–6 and winning the AFC North title, the Bengals lose 24–14 to the visiting New York Jets in a wild-card playoff game on January 9.

QUICK STATS

FRANCHISE HISTORY

1968—

SUPER BOWLS

1981 (XVI), 1988 (XXIII)

AFC CHAMPIONSHIP GAMES
(since 1970 AFL-NFL merger)

1981, 1988

DIVISION CHAMPIONSHIPS
(since 1970 AFL-NFL merger)

1970, 1973, 1981, 1988, 1990, 2005, 2009

KEY PLAYERS
(position, seasons with team)

Ken Anderson (QB, 1971–86)
Willie Anderson (OT, 1996–2007)
Eddie Brown (WR, 1985–91)
Cris Collinsworth (WR, 1981–88)
Corey Dillon (RB, 1997–2003)
Boomer Esiason (QB, 1984–92, 1997)
Chad Johnson/Ochocinco
    (WR, 2001–)
Anthony Munoz (OT, 1980–92)
Carson Palmer (QB, 2004–)
Ken Riley (DB, 1969–83)

KEY COACHES

Paul Brown (1968–75):
    55–56–1; 0–3 (playoffs)
Forrest Gregg (1980–83):
    32–25–0; 2–2 (playoffs)
Marvin Lewis (2003–):
    56–55–1; 0–2 (playoffs)
Sam Wyche (1984–91):
    61–66–0; 3–2 (playoffs)

HOME FIELDS

Paul Brown Stadium (2000–)
Riverfront Stadium/Cinergy Field
    (1970–99)
Nippert Stadium (1968–69)

* All statistics through 2009 season

QUOTES AND ANECDOTES

Was it a coincidence that the Bengals jazzed up their uniforms before the 1981 season, then went on to reach the Super Bowl? The new look included tiger-striped helmets, jerseys, and pants.

The Bengals received a shock and a setback in 1975 when Pro Bowl defensive tackle Mike Reid retired at age 28. Reid quit football to pursue a career in writing country music. He wrote songs for many country stars. Bonnie Raitt's version of Reid's "I Can't Make You Love Me" sold 6 million copies.

During the Bengals' long losing spell in the 1990s and early 2000s, *Cincinnati Enquirer* columnist Paul Daugherty wrote about the fans' misery. They began to feel it during summer training camp. "The point here is suffering," he wrote. "Suffering is the object. You get reacquainted with it in July, so by November, it's second nature."

In 1997, the Bengals exceeded 30 points scored in four consecutive games for the first time in their history. They tallied a remarkable 145 points in those games, winning three of them. The only problem was that the offensive onslaught meant little. The Bengals lost seven of their first eight games that season and were well out of contention by that time.

Bengals wide receiver Chad Ochocinco makes it clear that he enjoys playing the game. He recommends to players to "go out and play this game like you're a little kid again. This game is what you love to do. There should be nothing pressured about doing your job. It's what you grew up doing and always wanted to do. Just go out and play like you're a little kid again."

GLOSSARY

American Football League

A professional football league that operated from 1960 to 1969 before merging with the National Football League.

archrival

An opponent that brings out great emotion in a team and its players.

berth

A place, spot, or position, such as in the NFL playoffs.

contender

A team that is considered good enough to win a championship.

draft

A system used by professional sports leagues to select new players in order to spread incoming talent among all teams.

enshrine

To place into, such as the Pro Football Hall of Fame.

franchise

An entire sports organization, including the players, coaches, and staff.

inconsistent

An inability to play at the same level for a period of time.

media

Various forms of communication, including television, radio, and newspapers; the press or news reporting agencies.

mediocrity

The state of being average.

respectable

Highly regarded or well thought of.

rookie

A first-year professional athlete.

stingy

In football, a defense that is difficult to score or move the ball against.

FOR MORE INFORMATION

Further Reading

MacCambridge, Michael. *America's Game: The Epic Story of How Pro Football Captured a Nation.* New York: Random House, 2004.

Mersch, Christine. *Cincinnati Bengals History.* Mount Pleasant, SC: Arcadia Publishing, 2006.

Wheeler, Lonnie. *The Road Back: The Cincinnati Bengals.* Wilmington, OH: Orange Frazier Press, 2006.

Web Links

To learn more about the Cincinnati Bengals, visit ABDO Publishing Company online at **www.abdopublishing.com**. Web sites about the Bengals are featured on our Book Links page. These links are routinely monitored and updated to provide the most current information available.

Places to Visit

Cincinnati Bengals Training Camp
East Campus Athletic Complex,
Georgetown College
Georgetown, KY 40324
502-868-6300
Bengals practices are free and open to the public during training camp in August.

Paul Brown Stadium
One Paul Brown Stadium
Cincinnati, OH 45202
513-621-8383
This is where the Bengals play all their home exhibition, regular-season, and playoff games. The Bengals play eight regular-season home games every year.

Pro Football Hall of Fame
2121 George Halas Drive Northwest
Canton, OH 44708
330-456-8207
This hall of fame and museum highlights the greatest players and moments in the history of the National Football League. As of 2010, two players affiliated with the Bengals were enshrined—offensive tackle Anthony Munoz and wide receiver Charlie Joiner.

INDEX

About the Author

Marty Gitlin is a freelance writer based in Cleveland, Ohio. He has written more than 25 educational books. Gitlin has won more than 45 awards during his 25 years as a writer, including first place for general excellence from the Associated Press. He lives with his wife and three children.